THE OTHER ALTAR

THE OTHER ALTAR

POEMS

Nicholas Gulig

The Center for Literary Publishing
Colorado State University

For information about permission to reproduce
selections from this book, write to
The Center for Literary Publishing
attn: Permissions
9105 Campus Delivery
Colorado State University
Fort Collins, Colorado 80523-9105.

Printed in the United States of America.
Library of Congress Cataloging-in-Publication Data

Library of Congress Cataloging-in-Publication Data

Names: Gulig, Nicholas, author.
Title: The other altar : poems / Nicholas Gulig.
Other titles: Other altar (Compilation)
Description: Fort Collins, Colorado : The Center for Literary Publishing,
    Colorado State University, [2024]
Identifiers: LCCN 2024029627 (print) | LCCN 2024029628 (ebook)
ISBN 9781885635914 (paperback) | ISBN 9781885635921 (ebook)
Subjects: LCGFT: Poetry.
Classification: LCC PS3607.U5453 O84 2024 (print) | LCC PS3607.U5453 (ebook)
DDC 811/.6--dc23/eng/20240705
LC record available at https://lccn.loc.gov/2024029627
LC ebook record available at https://lccn.loc.gov/2024029628

The paper used in this book meets the minimum requirements of
ANSI/NISO Z39.48-1992 (Permanence of Paper).

for Fon

After a long time of light, there began to be eyes,
and the light began looking with itself.
—Ronald Johnson, *Ark*

O, the grieving vowel / zero, the mouth of astonishment
—Andrew Joron, "The Cry at Zero"

You are an altar of darkness. . . .
— René Char, "To Renew"

CONTENTS

Recently, my eyes have started, the garden darkening, a swarm of nightbirds rising
in the ghost-blue northern corner of the evening,

darkening. It is getting difficult
to tell exactly

where the edge of sleep
begins to blur

and where the silence of another
morning turns the inscape

of my utterance
to prayer. Fled is that music, tragic-

gestured, and fled again the name behind the song
that causes it.

Is there an altar here? There is an altar.
In light, the noise of light. In noise, the field the light records

I.

IN THE WAKE OF GRIEF, CREATE THE DIFFERENT LEVELS OF YOUR ALTAR.
THESE LEVELS REPRESENT THE EARTH AND AFTEREARTH AND SKY.

FIELD OF BOOK

A blue door opens in the wilderness—Walking through it.
Waking in the ruins

       of the book. A page of holes to intersect the world is outer lit.
                   A line of trees in which

///

Terror-struck // the ground
abruptly punctured.

Approaching over time a path of matted grass inverted early sky.

             The mediated leaves // their structure—
                  What is there to give?

///

Out of witness, into. The book emerging. The false dominion of the eye, emerging. Can still imagine it. Cinder-knit and scar. I continued counting. The sky was less than seven, less than absolute. For years I turned your voice into a ghost-voice, half mute, the agency of spring. Should it matter, then, the ground that loses magic when we speak? It loses nothing. Without your help, I've gotten used to spacing out the seeds. If I begin again from this vicinity, if we begin. There used to be this wooden bridge above the river

///

Beyond the book the burdock interrupted   underfoot. This path

a scrawl of branches left to drag a form across
and vanishing. The river

causing river   causing scrape. What is water for but placing in
                                                                or following?

I cup the filthy
liquid in // my hands. A map

                                                            my maker // gave
                                                                  the wind

///

In what direction, kneeling and not knowing. An unstable interplay between
positions, the light the book defines as crises turns back without escape. Here, an
exorbitant awakening unfolds beyond circumference. We were a garden once. The
ugly infinite. Every circle is a season, is a hole

///

Asterisk—The sky let down. I was meaning to make sense.
No one // rescued,

nothing left. Accepting
landscape as a monument, a structure resurrected

out of—the field I have for nearly half my life
returned to, leveled

and/or gutted. Believing
what is visible, a cold proclivity. Together we // are precipice.

When pressed against

               (a body feels dissimilar // is small

///

Every morning the words become a river ending in my mouth. I imagine you
are near me. Depending on the season, depending on the year, the book is what
subtracts us. Either way, it feels impossible to draw the world around your name
without remembering. We are disconnected perfectly. Errorlight, for instance, is
the vacant space beside a person sleeping in a field. Today the day is silver. I do
not believe it. If I am honest, I am here

///

If I am honest, I am here. The pattern of the wound is that I love you.
The way that it, the book, surrounds us

almost totally, a text through which to tell
the world remains adrift beyond

the edge of speech
to alter. Come September,

the air through which
the words describe

their voyaging destroys itself in half-
light. I had forgotten.

The weight of what the field has left within me
living, its shape

and resonance, a form that bends
the branches low enough

to tear what's rotted there
and eat it. The days, their awkward aperture. Blue, the blue dark

                                        opening. Overwhelm me.
                      There's something moving through me like // a song

///

And so

the song

itself

is silence

ever

in us (and

so the

silence is

itself

a sound

surrounding

II.

DECORATE YOUR ALTAR. SURROUND THE IMAGES OF THOSE YOU'VE LOST
WITH LIGHT. PLACE YOUR EARTHBOUND OBJECTS CLOSEST TO THE FLOOR.

BOOK OF WEAPONRY

Once, I held a stranger's rifle in my hand and walked alone into a moving field
of switchgrass, a sea of dead machinery abandoned at the edges, in the light.

In the center of the field, I propped a book I loved against a tree stump. The
wind rose up. The pages turned and stopped.

It was not unusual, the far hills glinting silver.
The book was there.

Believing in my name, its porous order, I picked the weapon up
and faced the distant language

of another. For an afternoon, I did this, a world within
the world that I imagined

brightening // in the vibrant after-
math of violence,

$$\text{the noise of forms reorganized, sent back}$$
$$\text{to me in drifts.}$$

Over and over, the book turned back into a flower. The hills became themselves
beyond themselves. The field bloomed up

$$\text{around me // like an empire}$$

1.)

Even now, there is no escaping it. The landscape opens in a book I haven't written and utterance retreats upon a path of gravel leading backward through the suburbs. One must try again and cannot say it. In the long dilapidation after tragedy, it is difficult to render the blue stairs ascending slowly in a mind whose body bends to noises, a poisoned mathematics in the bone. One must weigh their name against the muffled sound of others. Thus, the restless violence of the margins. And thus again the page

2.)

Lukewarm and capable of love, I have not invented music. The sound I make is that which overwhelms the prospect of a lack. Every morning, I try and fail to name the singer after my name. One is told of nothing

3.)

Because the moon tonight above the riots is the color of bad cocaine, the incongruent wealth the sky portends is only partially visible and the world remains a word whose synonym is *born*. All hail the bright emergence of these events, the stalled philosophies, the aesthetics common to the cathedrals of the 14th century. In prose, it grows difficult to fertilize a purpose. Among the blooming fragments of my youth, my face is faint and docile. Octagons connect against the distance. Parallelograms of stars, their imperfect reticence surrounding even he, the man whose face is colony, passing through me like a hiss

4.)

The noise of light I notice most surrounding each of us amounts to an emasculated nighttime sky. Memory is plastic, lukewarm. What is happiness? What are stars? Blinking back the dust, a different empathy replaces the incapacitated structure of our care. This is better oxygen. The city burning in the distance flits its inconsistent light against the desperate whiteness of our politics. Here, in the here, I place my failing language in a woodstove. A new September reddens in the molten center of the old

5.)

Without the risk of self-exposure. Without apology, or circumstance, or ache, the laurels upon which rest the dormant struggle of the leaves this autumn in a place I didn't choose to live in, their irrelevance and awkward grace, a patchwork covering of yellows. In the sea of dying grass that trims the yard around my house, I hold my daughter's hand as though it were an anthem. Aberrant cacophony. Death of the pastoral. Every time she picks a flower up and drops it, the petals spool into their shadows. We name them *Everything we've lost returns to us.* We press our ears against the ground and listen. We hear the blue-black bark of capital

BOOK OF SPRING

In daughterlight, like altarsong, another year distends its hybridized epiphanies.
Every night I dream my mouth around a plastic stone and sing.

These are the roots that clutch,
and this is the empty jar of their dominion,

wilding my sight. Awake again, a god I don't believe in
alerts me to the purple shadow cast across the kitchen counter by a spoon.

Love like an even number. I count the days until I'm future. Found
geography, my crooked grammar. Tell me in another language we are home

DESTROYER

Somebody says "yes." Not a soul so much
as something somewhere
other. Blurred
by brightstar, blurred by breath.
Chances are the world's what's ever offered
inward where
it's worse. A word within
a word, but what
surrounds it? No matter, whatever is
is sure to skip a beat
beyond my reason. The center spills too deep,
the still-far-maybe-beauty of the day.
Here is where the world
of things becomes impossible: the wrung-out
speech-thread hanging loosely
like a tooth-root. Un-
subtractable and scattered,
is it true our hollows coalesce,
a nest of inner endings
ending over in the unlit, threadbare
terrors of our rooms? We abandon everything,
and yet the space between us
blossoms outward like a zero opening its mouth
to swallow. That I have said
to you, "I need you." That you have said, "I'm here"

PRAY / TELL

For months, I wanted to take you to the wrecking place.
The light goes shaking there
and enters. In unison, down below
the fury and the beauty.
Lift me up and I will take you back
to anywhere that you remember
fondly, a field of rock
encrypted in your neck,
the world the wind
goes killing in, an actual locality.
It doesn't matter. Then,
when the letters of our names
are stitched together, almost
singular, it does. In this, the spell the weather casts
can cull at will the altar left to rot
atop the mountain. There where the water doesn't touch.
Can cast us thus ashore

DOOM SCROLL

Inhabited by dry spell, death bell.
The words turn off

without a whimper.
Every pulse

a syllable, every sound
a name erased

beyond its outline
on the sidewalk. A polemic mathematics

in the breeze. Redlined
in its history, the neighborhood

turns loose a different ground
from which to offer

witness. A woman
screams across the open border

of my daughter. Everyone
drives trucks. Without my implements

I walk alone across the secret
chemicals of grass

weeping in the patch-
work wealth

of the community. Hello, Officer.
Officer, hello. I dream of song and water

OMMATIDIA

In Keats's letters, the poet makes a specter of his aesthetics. Beauty should obliterate. As the riots burn in Minneapolis, I plant bee balm with my daughter in our yard. Because my friend in prison helps white supremacists write letters to their lovers and blinks himself to sleep, the police lights rising from the streets like little tongues beyond the dead insistence of their song upend the dumb capacity for grace. What must we forgive? To see a single flower in a field of other flowers, Keats insists that we abandon our identity. The lynching ruptured everything. To sustain the colony, a worker bee goes forth in early light and lingers. Sitting in the grass, we listen, the drone of tiny wings adrift between the patchwork patterning of violets, a kind of language glittering. At first, my daughter is afraid. When the open field between a thesis and its antithesis evaporates, Keats insists the arguments regarding art begin to dovetail in the mind. I want to think that he is right, the light of a convergence arriving on an altar I imagine centered somewhere in me like a soul. The city burning on a livestream while I send messages to friends illuminates my living room. When she pushes seeds into the dirt, my daughter asks if she is hurting it. A violent brightness casts a dark catastrophe across the wall. Capable of seeing ultraviolet light, the sun despite the clouds, the compound eyes of bees are covered with tiny follicles that sense the wind's direction. A disquisition, not dispute, on a myriad of subjects strikes me. I try to write a letter to my friend and find myself among a numb cacophony of distances, admitting my mistakes. What is true enough to render? This, for Keats, is the burden of the mystery, a liberating doubt. When my daughter asks if cops are bad, I grab her hand and say that in the morning we'll check to see if anything has sprouted. This pursued through volumes eliminates the call of all consideration. How beautiful the retired roses folding over in the night-wind, breaking. How fact and reason seem to fall away, my faith in people, the pistil and the stigma and the seed. When the workers first emerge, their hair is edged in silver and their wings are soft, paper-thin and crumbled. I tire early in the aftermath and think it sad that the specific composition of ommatidia varies between organisms, the world appearing differently as a matter of blind mechanics. When I drive across the country to see my friend in the Elkton Federal Correctional Institution, I stand in a line of children in the jail yard waiting with their mothers to see their dads. All of us are earthdark. Without poetry, I find I cannot exist, says Keats. And so I feel myself suspended in a landscape made of years and long apologies. In the prison cafeteria, my friend says the thing that shocks him most is how illiterate the inmates are. Queen bees brood their eggs like birds and place them in a pollen ball. When my daughter comes home from school, she asks if the police would ever hurt her mother and then we sit in silence. The silence ruptures us, a thing we cannot see that enters slowly through the ear and lingers, a wilderness approaching the immediate emergency of wreck, not a self so much, a subject. Thus, the music of the poem is what the mouth becomes when language leans into uncertainty. Landscape is imaginary. Every morning, when I wait in line in the Luther Elementary parking lot among the other parents dropping off their kids, I count the thin blue line police flags plastered to the metal bumpers of their trucks. Colonies exist to feed the queen's demand for sweetness, and this, too, is a kind of

silence lingering. I want to tell my daughter about the summer I was seventeen in Minneapolis, a punk show at a venue called the Bomb Shelter, how the cops came in and punched the brown kid standing next to me. In my memory, my mind goes blank on impact, my body acting on its own. For the first time I find myself beyond myself, the crowd erupting all around me and spilling out onto the streets of the same precinct burning on my phone today some twenty odd years later. I want to tell her that my friends together picked me off the ground and took me to the hospital, but instead I tell my students that the poet is at once the possessor and the possessed, the colonizer and the colonized, and that for Keats, language, when it is working, takes away your name. It surprises me to learn that bees have five eyes, three of which see only ultraviolet light. Maybe this is beautiful; vision is diverse. O for a life of sensation rather than of thought. Every autumn, the flowers we have planted start to fall apart, folding inward toward a center that is only partially there. My friend is out of prison. He's married now and has a daughter of his own. Every month he sends me records in the mail with little notes explaining his experience of song. Since an image from the compound eye is created from a set of independent elements, bees can only see that part of the picture directly there in front of them. It is difficult to know the world as someone other than yourself, to sense through nothing more than shadow there is in you a garden somewhere planted by a stranger, where the spirit you imagine passing through you glides against another person's body like a ghost. Keats believes that if the poem does not come naturally, like leaves to a tree in spring, it should not come at all. The riots rise and fall around my daughter like a century. The average lifespan of a worker bee is six to seven weeks. My dreams do not relieve me. In time, as the workers cross the distance from one flower to another, heading home to feed the queen, their wings deteriorate, battered by a wind that used to carry them. Laughing in a pool of pollen-colored light, my daughter sings my name and arranges yellow petals in a circle at my feet. In the chamber of our maiden-thought, Keats forewarns a darkening. The police are everywhere. My daughter tells me I am standing in the sun

A BRIEF HISTORY OF THE PASTORAL

Beyond the sun it's not
resistance anymore the work // an axis thus subtracted

xenophobic weight, a garden
now a grave in both your hands // that shadow

///

tiresome without   a record, sir it isn't beautiful

at all the mind as it occurs

could be a place   and I believed you // ruin

///

thus supplanted effigy, or Eros like
I want the many

languages as though the whole
the world becomes

when praying hard it isn't
there as landscape

pissed upon in imagery // or rain

///

etched in plains of grass the lung a zero closing
pantheons of horses fuck

in waves converging instruments a place remembers
the city woke you up

///

formed to fit the lake's interior
as thing the rain

as reciprocity the street
pretends its houses

like abuse is not to permanence // that path is not

to hills there isn't
such a thing

///

impossible transparency // the eye a dispatch opening

///

rather melancholically the world turns back // into its edges

ion // agonies

of light

the pupil's infinite regress
through green

to disappear
the work of weeping // blue

///

there it is
I see it

it // that we as well
are here

are not enough against
or terrored through the maples disappear // in creases

recollected merely strange
in poetry like how a history distends

within a garden
settled there in the // effect

///

like capital against
the foothills, flaming // an angel disarrayed

for now the forms of
houses moor

themselves within
the book imploding outward // error-struck

///

touch your finger to // the radius my love as crypt believing
zones of light

and hollow // now // a dank
cacophony

of voices interrupt the varied radicals of blue
arcadia the fields are getting off

///

a mouth is not a wilderness
I'm listening

///

desire is to chrome and absolute the languages

exist as silver
extending past in opposites a miracle that anything is here

at all // that any
thing is un-

corrected, existing
there the center bathed in paint

a burning sword extends in light
of the Americas // it could be said

and has been // if one has learned to writhe within
the lull of this

catastrophe, Dear Colony, the book
is not the song that I

had dreamed within myself // beyond myself
I promise

DREAMSONG OF THE ARTIST AS AN AUTUMN NIGHT

Read as a tradition, the leaves did not transgress,
were not what I imagined
being in the autumn of, or song.
Still, I felt their weight
appreciate. From them I made a world,
a living sculpture framed by arc, and ache,
and agony. Forgive me.
Thinking I had every right,
my language turned an untuned circle
in the air. The circle burned. Clouds

became their images. In an unkempt corner
of the sky, an inscape changed by smoke
accumulated. Terrified,
I traced the smoke's unfinished
thickening across the canopy, the death-
felled letters of the leaves,
whatever color or cliché, a spilt vocabulary scattered.
Everywhere around me, a trace of gray
I asked across the field
above me, my breath began again

beyond the scope of symmetry, a dark conglomerate
of stars. What is left to constellate?
But for the vagrant company of making,
I made alone each far-off fleck
of light a self surrounded by its progeny,
wept and was delivered inward.
I taught myself to pray. A little god
I spelled without an alphabet appeared,
approaching dignity and lacking
definition. In her I learned the names of others.

They, like me, were lonely. Naked,
enraged by our arrangement,
startled, staring out,
we screamed and were replaced.
Our scream became me.
Almost orderly, the light the stars announced
announced their dominance,
a narrative in which a pure amount
of mourning, a memory erased, arose and rendered equally
the night I quelled within myself

and verified. I was so villainous.
I loved myself too much. There, without philosophy,
I screamed again and felt within
a distant singing fall beyond the able tenor
of my reach, illuminating
nothing. A new darkness
swarmed around me.
I was impressed. From where I stood,
a man no more among the pitch and stretch of shadows
patterning the path's

unsteady margins, I heard myself
a record overturned
within the ruins of an artwork, speaking.
The wind, what was it,
wilting? It was western, so I left it.
The leaves, they too arose
and fell away from me
in drifts. They startled everything.
The stars burned red against their architecture

PRAY / TELL

Recently, the stars have started to go out,
the garden darkening, my voice
gone grave again
and lessening. I put my mouth upon the sand,
but the sand is made
of light, so I take my face away.
It's not supposed to be like this.
I put my wrist against my other wrist
and nothing happens.
The sky moves further out, blue,
then more than blue,
then black. As if the land was not
itself or even terrible.
When our minds go spilling
back and forth across the hard horizon,
irregular and changed, the song you were becomes
a colder version of
the sun, the shards of glass we strung
with copper wire from the trees, small jewels in which the light
had space enough to twitch

III.

FOR WHAT DO THE DEAD STILL THIRST?
THE JOURNEY TO THE AFTEREARTH IS FAR.

THE END OF APRIL

A blue hallucination, the rain tonight
upon the shed roof spells
a new vocabulary. Everywhere
the young are restless
in their dark encampments,
performing the important artwork
of the heart. It grows difficult to feel alive.
The police are gathering. The dead
in Palestine are gathering.
And so the far-off voices of the living
organize in ardent harmony
across the lost semester of the night.
What are we who teach them
learning? I am trying to remember. Gaza is book

SOME MYTHOLOGIES

Radial. Un-limiting except
that we abbreviate
the center. Isolated Brightness,
the book exists that I

must write to keep from you a narrow
definition. Star of Order where
the Names of Things
repeat until it isn't possible

to listen. In a closer world
the word for *cancel* is
accept. I am going to the garden left
in snow among the field

we couldn't harvest. Beautiful
unless. The light
is ghosting through
the river, the river's glint

///

Symmetries of Grain,
of Attar, the next belief will harbor
only momentarily.
Call it, then, the opposite, the post-

metallic taste of rain from off
the shed roof. I miss
the hiss of you. In motion
pressed against

and growing upward
into. Heaven happens when
you fear it. Clearly, I am enemy.
Do you remember

ways the buckshot scattered
cleanly through
the living? Low Star, Dead
Star, Night

///

Adjacent structures
lived in, we were not ourselves
among the even
ruins. Could almost taste

the fire having burnt
the walls away
discretely, illumined from the
center moving

up. Not a soul
so much, but rather I
have seen you
working in the strangest space.

Cloud of Other caught without
your star among
the singular. Believe that I am with you,
seeding wreck

///

Bravely known, the spirit rips apart.
Canceling the old
growth. Would that you
and I had faith

enough to argue freely
which of us
possesses here an
actual account. Seed of Plenty

crushed between a black stone carved
into a circle and
a red stone cracked into
a square. I go the way my father

tore to pieces. Disconnected from
the beautiful, the road
is lined with spaces
left by elm trees taken in the flood

///

Progeny of We, should it surprise us
here the light in which
our implements have worn out
has yet to be

collected? A parliament of plastic
owls haunting in
the rafters, a row of forms
that we have glued with feathers from

the roadkill. In you, their voices go
recorded. Amble up
the hill. Loadstar
blinking off as if to goad us

past a rational surrender. Do not
repeat it back
to me, the words for more than
what is northernmost. Cindering the Death House

///

Fear in the form of the abstract
rendered back to leaf-
like, flower-shaped. In this, our figures
rearranged already

into names whose origins
refuse us. Blue is what the ocean.
Algae bloom
and witness. Faith in that

which falls apart
on impact. Crush the little
worlds together. Unreal Avenues
of Homes

within whose light
the structure of
a room is prone to not
collapse unless an open window

///

Narrowing the doorways of
the temporary, found
geometries. In the kitchen sink
I am washing off

the dirt. Are you
near me? After surfaces, the night.
Once my lover took
me hunting. We shot at books,

the woods in mid-December
ringing. The sky propped up and
threatening. Is dead?
Emerge against my body

your current work. Philosophy of
Witness, please. It hurts
to look at you when
all I see I know that I am seeing through

///

Windowless, the room is a field
on fire. Burn Song, keep us
coming back. Is this correct, the crickets
clicking in the porchdark

look to take from us
our sixth and seventh breaths?
In the Lesser Garden there
are statues we

erected, hoping it would rain.
It isn't raining.
At night a multitude of insects flit
the empty ether, inner-

lit. Grab your favorite hatchet.
Groan of No One
echoed overhead. Hack the branches into pieces.
Glue the ugly petals to the trees

///

In a closer world, the next move would
be obvious. The stars align
but only when
the temple. Deconstructed out

of scratch, a gathering. That I
can see from here discordant constellations.
Believe in them as I do not
myself. In the house an aching built

the first to go are known
as either Orison, or
Surrender. In us, the clouds and what
the clouds depreciate.

Hope in owl form. A lake in which
the water where
we're true. Enough to disbelieve the branches.
Reorganized, the leaves

///

Grave of the Broken.
Grave of Light.
I am not that no. That you are
not. Can't

cancel. Looking up, the trees
erupted red and
budding. In new positions calling
into question, why

are you, what for?
In the Middle House Abandoned.
At the Edge of Godless Creek.
A black stone I

have centered in
my hand. Don't throw. Grave of the Perennial
Retreat. As in an inner
distance giveth over. Asking it away

PRAY / TELL

In the space around your joy the darkest
thought is bettered by
your asking of the dark to carve a path
behind you, a doorway in a forest
painted blue. Lift
the branches up. Clash and grind
and scatter. Above us,
nothing less is still enough
to spin a wish into
the sky. Here, where even stones
are eyes to set within
our heads if we arrange the symbols
underwater. Constructing
answers out of clamor, out of scratch.
So much as we have known,
your throat within the house
like however many ghosts, an absolute in which the faces of the dead
are windows. Facing upward, one of them is open

A HISTORY OF SLEEPERS

1.)

What I remember mostly isn't past. The night goes ticking through the clouds
and what surrounds them stills my rough vocabulary.

I can't recall my calling.

Incomplete and buried, the years evaporate, a series of incredible explosions
dispositioning the angle of the human jaw.

Every day, a ghost day. Every garden,
secretly a grave

2.)

That I have loved and failed to love, forgive me. There are those whose memories
are latched, whose eyes can only close

partway. I
am one of many

who sleeps alone
and dreams of speech preceding me through trails

of smoke beyond the autumn
breathing of the yard

LITERARY CRITICISM

For *The Book of Smoke* was done with me.
For I hadn't finished

reading, nor had I tracked
the crooked path by which I came to recognize

myself. Among the strange cacophony
of colony, make no mistake:

the map I've kept no longer
guides me through

my narratives. For outside, a lone magnolia disappears
into the shadow of a better tree

and America collapses. How is one
to navigate the dark inertia

of their suffering?
Among the many predicates

for dawn, my father is a ghost bone
carried in a dog jaw. For I am not myself

nor am I starting over
among the dumb assumption

the dark is not the dark
I read about. For what is love

except a bloodstar rising nightly?
What is light except the distant thrum of hovering?

SPECTACLE

A light in the woods evaporates, is almost possible, the sky—
irrelevant unless exactly—spoken into

spirit, spire—to say to you
I can't, not really, here—in unilateral

dimensions—too pretty to believe in what
I can't succumb

beyond the net of anything
is possible—the glint of mathematics

in the trees, a little
symmetry—is not the self

such blueness—dilapidated brightness, a voice in the leaves & therefore

overwhelming—verifiable & struck—
& ugly—the sky becomes

vocabulary—no silt unless imagined—dioxide now
that the interior

reflects—a lake of light
& oil—black silt—no shore except

that one must drive a thought through something honest—
it isn't accurate—when I count

the trees into a forest I forget myself
among the very many

branches—a series of
a series of—approximating nearness—very pretty—seven—

the leaves do not add up
not perfectly—the green the grass is

wet with weeping—nest
of nothing where, despite the bright veracity of never, no

not really—no—not nothing—the branches only almost—singing—
in unison below the fire &

the beauty—meet me in
the field's entirety—how terror-filled & full

of grief that we, affected,
are—

the trees where you are—here—the light
where I am—there—

bright moss clinging near the stream edge—lichen—scattered on the rocks
without arrangement—a grave

in every opening—when touched the surface of the self
recoils—a world

of photographs, what for—it is taking centuries—by way of cutting

down—& soaking
& pasting back together—bleach—the always altered—

if poetry proves anything it proves that there are parasites of many sizes, selves—
myself the woods behind

the house that hope becomes
my vacant faith—the effect of which

is dialect—& drone—
& deadstand—a world of leaves the light of what

does one belong to—here—if not
spectacular, if still

HOPE IS A DARK FLOCK RISING

In Dickinson's 314, the poet turns her hope into a bird. I'm almost 40. Because they've started coming back, I imagine this desire blurs into a horned lark. It's February, cold, and local outlets announce the presence of the virus in Wisconsin. Such is the power of metaphor. According to reports, the patient walked alone into a hospital. My body slows into its history. In periods of lasting isolation, the theory of allopatric speciation contends that over time some birds phenotypically respond to their geography. How are you doing, my daughter writes in a letter to her friend. Separating species, this variance in habitat demands a new vocabulary. Their symptoms were consistent. In the open field between an object and its import, language clutches with its ghost hand at the air. Metaphors conflate. For Dickinson, the bird that hope becomes is either prior to or after speech. A thing with feathers that perches in the soul. These symptoms include recurrent coughing, fever, and fatigue. An endless, inner singing. Often, the body aches and does so deeply, a pain that lasts for days and echoes in the muscle, in the bone. At first, I paid

no mind. If birds of the same type are kept apart for long enough, they cease to see themselves in others of their kind, their common song no longer a reunion. In some cases, the lips and face turn blue from lack of oxygen. The song moves in and out of us. Spreading exponentially. In a post-pandemic world, the exchange between a symbol and its referent now requires the strange catastrophe of breath, what Dickinson calls a storm. Not long before their fever, the patient had been to see their family. Hope, it seems, cannot be parted from the maelstrom. My first thought, if I remember, was not a thought at all. I heard it in the chillest land—and on the strangest sea. A blue silence rose within me. Every day, at three o'clock precisely, the children in my neighborhood stand alone in separate driveways and yell each other's names across the boulevard. My faith in art is that the bird exists as an insistence and can and will disrupt the context of its singing, its small voice passing through an air we now imagine poisoned. Crossing continents and oceans, one presumes the patient had wanted to see the faces of their loved ones. To be a form held tight against another. I, too, desire to be a form held tight against another. Every night I grab a can of beer from my refrigerator and talk nostalgic with my friends. The virus is a line of air connecting us to people we'll never meet, whose names occur in languages we'll never speak. Our tongues are dark. Our lungs our ravenous. The Department of Human Services is operating with an abundance of caution. We are older now, and lonely. The existence of extrinsic barriers obstructs the call-like variance of our transmissions. It is difficult to think of hope in Dickinson's work without remembering that when I read it, I find myself beside myself, unspooled in a different wilderness. As if for the first time, we are learning how to see each other, our faces glitched and framed by our computers. It is getting difficult. Often, her language falls apart, the frequent dashes suturing the starts and stops of fragments, a kind of calling out from deep within the terror of a pause. The patient is being monitored. In moments of extremity, the song arrives as if the storm had beckoned it. Dear Cubby, my daughter writes, I wish that we could play. Here, where no one is themselves, we're telling the story over, night by night. The first death, then the second. Our language loosens in the air. The friend my daughter writes to is the daughter of a man I've known since we were children, so when they set their letters in the mailbox, it feels like we do too, our history returning across the landscape, a time and place no longer present moving through our kids. All of us are breathing. The structure of our lungs expands to house the living remnants. My daughter stares beyond the window. Here, in Wisconsin, the first returning migratory birds perch on the snow-bright stalks of goldenrod. Sheltered though we are, our hope is that in which we speak to stitch ourselves together. Dickinson was wrong; this requires everything. The patient is now at home. Months before it's spring, the horned larks gather in dark flocks, picking through the ice and stubble, searching for hidden seeds. This is their geography. When frightened, the flock alights as one, a single entity twisting swiftly, their lisping callnotes disappearing in the half-imagined distance of their song

---

"Dickinson's 314" refers to the version of "'Hope' is the thing with feathers" from *The Poems of Emily Dickinson*, edited by R. W. Franklin.

BOOK OF TALK

To live again we choose a language,
use it early in the aftermath
of evenings, listening. Do our instruments
instruct us, tell us everything
we've lost returns to us
through shade? To speak again
we shoot a book I love
upon a wooden spindle
placed behind your house
and spell the disappearance
of a word both in the world
and from it sounding
far. It's beginning to be
that time again. The snow
in isolated flecks across the yard
arrives, another year
in this, the somehow middle
of a life gone by
too quickly. Home is where
we're here again, a song
we've learned by
living it. Even when we leave,
Wisconsin glistens
in its insistence, the crawl
of seasons like a lover's breath,
and everything I wish
that I could sing
to keep our better years
abreast arises through me
with the quickness of
a wrist pulse. What I mean
to say is, *Yes.* Desire

is a room unto
itself. The stairs are crooked
and the stars that light
the floor are leaking,
spilling liquid
in the lacquered
dark. Even the
low moon's dress
hung out to dry
with nothing in it
frays its alabaster
threads beyond
the distant glowing
of the house. The world
is busy making
room for ghosts,
and everything I've said
to them returns to me
unmade. Let us wait to pray
until the words pronounce
themselves without us
and the snow accumulates
around our ankles
like a halo lowered
through the only
light there is to know
a person by. Someday soon
our kids will stand
where we do, telling stories
of the days their fathers
talked for hours over
music, the high notes flickering
like an absent faith
come back to guide us
through its wake. Grief remembers
everything. The dark is old.
The songs that we've exchanged

preserve our listening
in rooms. Somewhere else
you're making beautiful mistakes
and I believe you. Love
is thunderous. Our voices winter
like a memory in which the both of us
are younger, the struck expression of our faces
escaping through a painting of a window, on a wall

WEST WIND

Ancient in my asking, blue truths circumnavigate the dairy state.
Maybe I am dumb enough to sing.
As a long fall descends upon the continent,
a new emergency erupts
within the taut interiors of white men.
Just yesterday I watched a blue jay
peck apart an egg. Maybe the thin veneer of reason
isn't the firm stone ground
it used to stand upon. I am filled with questions for the dead.
How is it local birds do not erupt
in flame each time their call notes
vanish in the city's thickness? Are the two black rocks I threw
into the river, demanding violence
to the president, worth going in to save?
Just yesterday I watched my lawn turn brilliant
within a silver arc of water erupting upward
from a plastic Walmart sprinkler.
I called my mother and told her that I loved her.
A rainbow etched itself in air.
Maybe, when I'm older, I'll stop imagining
the policemen all have names
and walk alone for once into the shuddering
despair of the second half
of my existence. I no longer check my bank account.
Truth is, I know I'll never leave the incoherent structure of my history,
never draw my form around my form in chalk
or step beyond the limits of a language. In my left hand,
blue shells turn to shitty narratives. This sky is not the sky I learned about in song

THE RADICALS

Once I dreamt I was a woman. A dark blood
pushed its sentence past me, diachronically,
and the leaves were nearly
beautiful that September
in a city that I didn't choose
to live in. Power floats
like money. I was a woman,
barely, a lack of justice dripping
off me, almost sultry, sounding something
close to rain, or rather through it,
pouring. Language floats
like power, a pair of plastic jays in every other branch,
the tilt and color of a dark bird
ripping through a road-deer
rather lazily. I wanted very much a difference.
The leaves were red and masculine
and raw. Producing outpour,
the little sky through which
the echo of a bonebreak overcomes its use
in poetry no longer underwhelmed me
into agony. I gave it everything. I had the world
I was when I was not subservient
through which to render in the inky dusk a string
of pearls and brittle letters. Power floats
like theory. The sky was not a clearing,
the streetlamps pushing past
the branches' curve, a curse because the light
was almost natural, and how my thighs began to ache
a little when I screamed beyond
police. Fuck me to the rotten core, Aporia.
The stars are critical. There's something fishy thinking through me like a dove

BOOK OF FLAGS

The horizon of the poem
exists, a blue arc
flickering, and now the wilderness bleeds out,

distributing its rags
against the ground like what is not
an exit. Witness with me

or against me. In the brittle thicket
of an anthem, an ethics
leaves its mark upon the plastic

flowerwork of whiteness. I never loved you.
Violence is a list

DREAMSONG OF THE YOUNG CONDUCTOR

Despite the night's resplendent radio, its end
does not accept me. Left to my devices,
I turn on from far away
the fragrant distance of its music
nonetheless. Albeit beautiful,

the way the moment after orchestras
arranges strange applause
approaches an appropriate disfigurement.
Tonight, as I prepare to let
my thinking ring, the hands of men

grow tired at the freshly laundered edges
of their sleeves. Though no one leaves
themselves across the common dark,
the theatre fills until it doesn't.
My eyes descend upon

the bannisters. What is it that brings the masses
to their noises? Without them,
I am one of them. I trust myself too much
to love another maker
and must make do without a language

leaning through me like a history.
Soon I'll stand in silver isolation
on a stage. The world
in which it's difficult to care
does not forgive me, my half-face twisted

to a grin each time another's voice
protects my name by saying it,

and so I say again to all the gentlemen
in night-coats, the dusky ladies straightening
their gloves, *Welcome. This evening*

it is my honor . . . and then I raise my arms.
My coattails stretch and lengthen like the news,
its nearest region loitering, I fear,
is never music, although I listen when I'm hungry,
when I'm home. Just yesterday,

for example, in a place where I have never been
except within the wooden crawl
of a viola, a young man lit himself on fire,
hoping in the almost perfect presence of an end,
despite the rain he feared was coming, that it wouldn't

PRAY / TELL

As for this, the actual subtracting
of the attic from the stone
foundation, enter blindly and in love,
the space upon an altar
left for air. Keep your faith
in wreck. Even gods grow smaller
here, less quiet.
Kill the quiet when you speak
and then pretend it's not
the magic but the math that makes you
miss it. My enemy,
my empty. Forgive me if I shake,
here where the river edges
past us and draws back; I want
to cage a bird beneath
your dress and listen.
Mostly it is echo. Mostly drone
the music makes of us,
and so we make again in unison,
the dark and not dark stitched together,
a circle woven into other circles. Opened into, wound

GROVE OF MEANING

In the middle of September, after everything
we loved had ended, the day remained

a sound pronounced among
emergencies. It was almost

beautiful. A scrawl of voices shook an opposition
through the trees, and I believed them.

What is not forgivable?
Among the black metallic structure

of a language, imperfect
in the present tense, I called to you

across the open grove
and listened. Terror-struck and tethered

to each other, we lived and breathed and were surrounded
by our speaking. The leaves descended

like the inconsistent weather of the law. Our voices
carried them. Ungovernable, the sun, the sun, the sun

To write the book a second time, I shoot it. When my father dies, I leave the room and stand alone at the end of a long hall, looking down on Minnesota. I know of no other happiness, writes Oppen, but the mind rising into what is there. It's summer in the Middlewest and 10 are dead in Buffalo. I call a friend and weep into the telephone. A field of knee-high grass surrounds me. I lay the book against a tree stump. Confronted by police, the shooter removes his armor in a fluid motion close to grace. The hall is empty. He sets his weapon briefly against his chin and then surrenders. The switchgrass sways. Every time I stare along the rifle's spine and pull the trigger, buckshot scatters in the bright light. The pages separate; the book begins to pull itself apart. In the racist theory of replacement, men like me, women like my wife, children like my children, stand to disenfranchise white men. For Oppen, the failure of language to be transparent is a failure to move beyond the shipwreck of the singular, a falling short of love. I used to think there was no one I loved the way I loved my dad, but then I had a daughter. At night, I light a candle and tell his ghost I'm sorry. The echo of a gunshot slants against the hills. The book begins to blossom. Although his actions resonate beyond the single moment of their occurrence, rippling outward, the bullets proving that the borders of the self are porous, the shooter was alone. When my sister calls to tell me I need to make it home, I'm poor and living in a small apartment half a world away in Thailand. When I put the phone against my chest and hold it, I turn to the woman who is now my wife and the room begins to shrink itself around a silence the likes of which I know today my children will also have to someday navigate without me. In Jean Raspail's 1973 novel, *The Camp of the Saints*, brown immigrants band together to overrun the continent. My daughters scream each other's names and sprint across the yard. The weapon, heavy in my hands, the book unfurling upward. I haven't written since I've had kids, so when a girl I used to think I'd marry suggests we work together on a project, I'm afraid. In my memory, I set the rifle down and lay alone beside the book and let the light across my face go forth without the need to name it. For you and of you, I begin, I am growing in the cold stone a garden in my basement, and then the poem falls out of me like water. When my youngest daughter reaches for the picture of my dad I keep on a shelf above my records, she asks me what it means to die. The poem prescribes itself its ending, a silent litany of grief. My daughter pauses. Death, I say, is when a person turns just small enough to climb alone into the hearts of those they've left behind and live there. It is a place, Oppen writes. Nothing has entered it. Nothing has left. The depth of water pours from all its sources. My earliest memory is of a dream in which my father disappears into a painting of a ring of children holding hands that used to decorate my bedroom. In it, I'm alone and screaming out his name. When I wake up the scream remains, but this time he's sitting in the room beside me and saying it's OK, everything will be OK. Strangely, some thirty-odd years later, these same words promising my safety are the last I'll hear him speak. I cannot even now altogether disengage myself, Oppen writes. I pick the book up off the ground and carry it. As versions of white replacement theory overrun the continent, my daughter climbs into my lap, puts her head against my chest and says my dad's awake in there and wants to know if he can visit us in summer. When I can't write a poem I feel alone in a world of corporations, standing in a hall of endings, listening. The names of the dead according to their faces blur into the general onslaught of the news and disappear. I, too, like you, am guilty of forgetting. In *The Passing of the Great Race,* Madison Grant posits that genetic dissolution will cause the West to fall. Every night my daughter puts her face against my cheek and whispers in my ear. Rome begins to burn a second time, the ghost of Athens, all of Alexandria. The book is lighter now and larger. Because my dad will never meet my kids, I'm trying to remember him when he was young, but the older that I get, the more the form I apprehend appears increasingly transparent, his language failing him a day before his body does. I want to live forever so that my kids will never need to write a poem like this, but so does everyone, I think, and so my hope is dumb. My daughter kisses me and I promise silently inside myself that I'll remember the weight her face exerts against my own, the quiet pressure of her mouth a kind of music moving through me, blooming. In the garden of my memory, I guard the growing darkness of my grave and drag a branch across the wild grass and sing. My singing ceases. In the room my father's growing smaller in, I read to him until my shoulder slumps against his deathbed. I have not and never did have any motive but to achieve clarity, writes Oppen. My children sleeping in the other room appear to me the reason there is light. The absolute singular. The unearthly bonds of the singular. When he met my mother, I wonder if my dad imagined me, if at some point and only for a moment, I existed long before my body did. A single candle flickers near a picture of my father on an altar. The book I shot is now alive in this book. The light of the pages packed against each other exposes the new day

ALONG OUR MOUTHS, SING SOFT

For you and of you I am
growing in the cold

stone a garden in
my basement, rising near

your books, your little sprigs.
Your books, your little reachings—

My hope is that the sentence
finds you, blossoms

through its structure, somehow
summer, somewhere

inner, other than
and after, always after—

I remember once in winter
we were younger

and you, who were
you then to me

who said that every anger
stems from grief,

a kind of pushing
through the untilled blue

interior of loss, its litany of tiny silences.
It's getting difficult

to tell my children. Here,
where I am, there, where you are writing

in the Jersey dusk, your mother
in a fur coat

watering the lawn
and the shape your brother left behind

in photographs, a kind of language
I have placed

inside the students
passing through the rooms I work in now

and never write
myself except to say it here,

in this, to you: I wish
that you could meet them, Jane,

Diana, my children,
Lilly, if you could see them

pouring water in the cold electric
light beneath my home,

the living brightness
of their faces—we are making this

together: paper, pulp from little pieces,
seeds that you have sent

to me, to them, my children,
who have only ever listened to their father

saying, listen, look, a day will come
and you will need them,

stranger, former lover, friend I've met
in ink and image

still remaining, a red string
marking fracture, the future structure of a tree

I hope to live to care for. It's getting difficult.
My daughters hold your books

and read them, the oldest
to the youngest, the distance splitting open

like the little silences
of plant parts, sad nectaries.

There is a difference between
the image resurrected in my memory—

it's summer and you are standing
in a yellow dress

weeping in the August garden
of our yard, searching

for our cat among the wilted squash leaves—
and history, that field we were

that never happened,
how saying it again today

arranges everything in ghostlight,
your mother squatting

in the kitchen of her parents' house,
rinsing herbs, the green stems

glistening like everything that's gone.
At night I sit alone

among my records, read aloud
and turn into a father

who used to be a writer.
I've almost all but stopped except

to tell my students, *Look, here
is where the poem*

is finally listening, and here, and here
where we are hungry

in the middle of a life. Theirs is a language dreamt
in explanation, expected lull

of rain, of rot which Jane insists
is love, is lullaby

the low birds drift upon
in song. Little Swallow of the Cliff,

how dare you? Mother of
a Thousand Lanterns, what does it mean

to prove yourself
to no one, to nothing

in particular? It's not too late.
I've cut the peppers, I've pushed the seeds in deep

and pressed the pulp across the screen
and waited: a heart of glass

is less transparent
than it seems. It's getting difficult.

If you were somewhere I could reach
despite the cage arranged

around the body's shape,
I'd feed you everything we've planted:

Little Flowers, Little Suns
whose light arises

in the ever-vaster pasture of the poem
I tried to turn into a book

for you and of you, but I couldn't get it right.
Love is difficult. The walls

are gray. The trees hear rumors
in a wind that speaks

the names of those we leave behind
by living. Little Palimpsest,

Little Song, what kind of grief
is this in which the words return to us as paper?

PILGRIM

If I believe again myself a different wilderness,
a blue wind sparkling

the under-dark
of trees, a simple fire

like an anguished language
in the endling season of the leaves

exposes the old millennium
of talk. Everything I lick

is mine. Young god,
these are not my circumstances.

Although I drag my hair
across the dirt and pray to no one else

who isn't, what is it
that startles me

into attention? The many voices of a stranger
drive a green cacophony

across the field within my chest
and rise. The wind is post-

existent, pre-imaginary. Night-
bird, Cloud-edge, Shore-

where-every-noise-becomes the-name-
that-I-discarded-

for-my-mother. In the loosened folds of evening,
my children wait for me and listen.

Will I return to them?
My likeness trembles on an altar, like a star

AMOR FATI

This is how I've loved: dark sky
above the garden
where you're buried,

bruise of wind
like language slipping
into grieflight, the drifting edge

of listening. Here,
where I am other than
and after, the incandescent wake

of every mercy I've been given
clears the myriad complexities
of ache, my only ardor,

error, like the bluest harbor,
the shoreline shaking
in the inconsistent weather of your name

BORDERWORK

Our being here together is the night-struck violet
plucked from an edge-blue curve of air.
The light does not absolve us.
Because we named our children
in the margins of a garden's darkness,

the white rose listens.
I love the thousand shades of you.
Every morning, our daughters sleep beyond themselves
in dayglow. The house grows quiet in their wake.
To the place where you should be

I lash the ache of every brightness
I've disfigured, the years that we have left.
Bury with me the bottom half
of fenceposts in the yard. Pack the loose dirt harder.
These days, I'm beginning to believe

that I belong here. Because we chose
to raise our children in the center of an empire,
the low grass glistens in the west
wind. At night, the sky-edge finds us staring at our hands.
It is easy to forget we left a world for this one

BOOK OF SHORE

Superior, by which I mean the lake was not
as much as we imagined
it, a synonym, or else the surface,
cold because the light
was catastrophic
in the distance, no, the water made of its
appearances, the presence of
a promise formed
the shore, the waves repeating
and repeatable. I had thought
that I was making
up, was therefore under it, the sky

was strange within
the world at once upon
but not itself
belonging. We looked away,
were other than
and then the day was not of what between us
edged, growing
into sand the dark dissolved
to something less
than brilliance, the wind within
itself a distance
yet again, a distance. I had to ask it

everything. Our voices
almost mattered
making sense, the lake is every
kind of blue today,
you said, it is
and it is cold, I know, but what will come

of it tomorrow. I can't
pretend what's left
that we without ourselves
are shaking, made of this
material. Or maybe it, what was it,
only mattered into, formed itself

from nothing new, a sound
I said, or else I only
listened to, or thought to try but couldn't
say existence is
an exit we have traced
our lives to find it
thus, the line the trees have made
behind themselves, green
and gray where people aged alone
in separate languages, the shade in which
increasingly their names
became mechanical, becoming difference,

always difference, as if no other shore of light
to hollow out or follow, no path
behind us leading each
unto each other here, where it, whatever is
is never certain, love, unless
alone that we are possible
in this, the unkempt
vacancies of how
between the beautiful and full
of loss, that I might reach for you
and find not only clarity, but solitude, a terror turned
to wonder, tuned to our despair

LYRIC

Beyond the new calamity of listening.
In a western arc of light

against the dumb imaginary wall.
Erected in the book

amid the earthbound quarrels
of the body, perishing

like thought, a vision of my children
thirty years from now,

the law of time, their faces
strange. What will I not recognize?

When the edge of speech releases me,
finally I'll collapse. Inside the book again beside them

OF GENESIS

The origin of every book is loss.
There is not a word

in the beginning
and language always listens

to its end. Tell me
what has left its mark

upon the names you give to stars
you cannot see,

and I will try to break the sentence
into something

strange enough to trust. Look,
the world is blue

as death down here already. The air is poisoned
by our breath. It is getting difficult to teach our children

how to speak by speaking

IV.

ATTEMPT TO SIGNIFY THE HEAVENS.
CONSIDER MARIGOLDS AND LAVENDER IN JARS OF WATER.
EVERY CANDLE GIVES ITSELF AWAY.

BOOK OF LAKE

If there is a world, let me be in it.
—Joanna Klink, "Processional"

In increments, the book became itself

        beyond itself.
As when the world was water-

swept // the words dissolved among the reeds
and litter wrapped

    around—the wind as well, the lake unspooling
inward // like a discourse

///

Promised through, the air is overwrought and not released. Calamities of almost metal insects clicking in the bright. Halls we have forgotten. The painted rock of walls, that we are not ourselves. Every time the book begins again, the house that I've become collapses. Erupted off the tangible. A mind, a favorite sky, a future. These are the shapes of clouds adrift against the mountain, a wilderness of difference, a sentence. Undone among the constellated mess: evening, kingdom, flame. Upon the myriad of rooftops. Would that one could suffer further inward and recover. As if the diagnosis didn't matter. The way it isn't summer. What kind of finite? What kind of absolute bouquet?

///

Parenthetical, an amphora
of light conceived

as if the act of seeing
were enough—

myth and bioluminescence—
As children prone

to press the brightness
out // we painted.

The images
existing. Images

exist (I want
to show you // everything

///

The hardest part is parsing out
and speaking. Dust

collected on the plastic
jacket of // the book. Reconstructed

into logic, resurrected
into swell—the road that splits the shore in half

down which
the trees are beetle-

burrowed // dropping shade (a lake
I am that you surround me now that the interior reflects—

not catastrophe so much
as failure. In the sense of being

orderly. // And so I say the landscape is
my opposite. And so what is it that // I mean

///

A sense of the extravagant, this path of matted grass between the trees erases me

///

Despite the book and of it, a love of wilderness and not the place
itself, the startled deer

because they dragged their antlers
through, canceled

and/or kept
the far idea in tune

and out of
order. Immediate, the hills

in increments. "I wanted every mineral
to stay" in place the anti-

ontological in which
an absolute // catastrophe

///

Disfigured into symmetry while I was thinking, a landscape rendered into asking,
into ache. Paging slowly through the book. Both does and doesn't help, this

drift. Beyond a garden wilting in September, wanting to reach out, I clasped my hands around a weapon's wooden handle. The field was all around me, terror-lit. The water seemed approachable. *More than anything,* you said, *the inner deriving magnitude, the outer.* In the middle distance, believing something that I couldn't. Infant curl of fern

///

"Our bodies missing not intelligence so much
as argument." Inter-elemental

"does one thing and
the same,

is not dissimilar exactly." Gleaned and/or dismissed, the fraying
edges. Aster

in the shattered chaff
Milkweed,

burning // nettle.
The story goes

I need you. Cannot
not talk.

Although we have "decided
to become"

///

Abrupt solidity—and then to still continue
to describe // an inscape

interrupted—Therefore,
the field grew up

around me like
an empire, casting out across the pages

of my body. Images of grass
but not the grass // itself, "the weight that thinking bore"

///

"Flooded over, the river, then, is absolutely relevant."
Although it is

impossible—
Drag the bottom

as though a thought can only
almost touch it—

A shore of trees
emerging

out of witness. Out of having
the ability (the leaves

in motion. Make the
motion up

///

Single mind of

the leaf, the
stem

///

The branch. In water,
winter

///

A sky gone, the gray-blue
evening. Bird–

less distance. Mind
of the

horizon
interrupting

pitch, an auburn north the light
has startled

out // has left

///

Today the nightbirds interrupt the air above the fencepost. Between one place, where you are, and another. After harvest, after seed. We are not together as the single oak outside the house begins to empty and we are not together when it fills. Every distance has been rendered. The days are absolute. When I walk into the yard a multiplicity of insects flick their little lights incessantly. I flicker back.

Against the early dark, I plant the desperate parts, forgive me. As the river lowers, as the sumac reddens like a warning. The weather, good or bad, reverses every rage. Both is and isn't happening, this this. Larkspur in the far field bending. Belladonna writhing in the grass

///

Afterwards, an open space between
the separated pistils. The sun

against the gravel rounded under-
water. An octave

lower, there is
something verifiable

to locate, yes or no? Too pretty to believe
you, Spirit. The first word, not the

second. I am gutting out
the garden. (Take me closer to the lake

///

In the direction of the lake
I take you

closer. Together we
submerge

our wrists, the shoreline
lessening, leaving

sand. In the lake we turn to water
there beneath. We river

under. Deepening,
the water

warmer than I
remember

moves when we remove
our politics

///

The other day I said your name and very little happened. This winter I've been
singular. I stand sometimes in rooms where very little happens. What I mean,
I think, is yes. The trees are growing circular, the level of the water, lower. I owe
you more than I am able to erase. Forgive me if I have failed to follow perfectly
the line of sight gone out above and not below me. Snow is what a zero does.
Take me there and I will show you how, with little effort, to vanish through its
center

///

Spelled and/or distressed, the shallows
waded into I could almost

see the wind could feel it
changing on

the lake its surface
turned to writhing turned

upon the shore my heart gave
out gave nothing

back I swallowed hard the air came in // and left me

///

The air came in and left me: I wanted love.
I wanted love I thought to ruin
it without you meant within me nothing
less the far-off sound prolonged
in droves approaching
circular a zero hung a garland yes
around my neck in ice-
lit boughs of needles threading silver I
could not dissolve completely in you though
from far away in this defeat
inaccurate with both my eyes I tried

to echo back the stirring
earth within the imprint left behind to tell
the story clearly life has happened
here it can't return the shape
of fields we slept alone
inside of thinking how
and for and what
for who could not exist unless
in aftermath a bluer light was splayed upon
our bodies pulling
water there from the interior

a sea of green and black in both
our eyes our mouths
were tightly
wrapped in morning

vines could not believe the waves the un-
shored water offered
through to think we could in maybe stress
the matter further past
ourselves the other
matter waking now the field the almost
singular in which to still

believe the name you gave
to me material in winter more the world
that comes together in
your wake you drone behind you
leaving at the edges of
the shade your form it isn't clear to see
from this position stranded I
am tracing also here the face of stones
the sound of which
in snow your eyes
release the ground as I recall

///

Every summer we remember we are matter. Flattening the grass, the fact of having
happened in a field becomes itself the feeling of the field against us. Today I stood
and set the rifle down. Our memories are ugly. Walking through it, waking. Once
you held the mess of pages in your arms. High in the interior, if you take the care
to carve it, I'll cook the carcass in the pot before it rots. Thyme leaves drying in
the window, in the sun. Your reflection is a field on fire. Words are perforated.
There is little one can do to stop the clouds of pollen carried off the weeds

///

Insects dart the scrub brush. In what direction, kneeling
and not knowing. Crush of beetle-

husk, a hand.
The wind across

the lake in undulations, crippled
innards. The color of

the air is rust the water leaves, a lull of trees emerging out
of their // emergency

///

Barely verifiable, a thin black V of geese. A red truck and a black truck. In winter we were going back and forth between our separate houses. There wasn't radio. I held on and you did. A sudden form of violence in the snow, the headlights turning. Music made of window glass and gravel. The road was not the road was not the accidental edge. *The problem,* you insisted, *is that the book cannot contain one's thinking back upon it from an unspecific point on the horizon.* Letters in the sky, or numbers. The edge closed in around us

///

The edge closed in around us. Northernmost,
the stony path around the lake,

its water. Still, then not
as still, then stiller. Which of us will shelter?

Let the rock decide. Let it hollow out
the sound that most resembles

screaming. Blurred
in snow, the form of every element

the mind is turned against or into. A row
of exits, zero minus zero

minus ache. Exterior to error, the part of us which fills
the mouth with earth // with earnestness

///

Uttered into   a landscape
                    scraped

              by hand. Undoubtedly the mind
                    into a garden

turned. And the   community of
                          minds
              together (and the community

///

         In the present room, the idea

                    a person has
                    of other

                    rooms. In
                    the other

                    rooms, ideas
                    that other

              people // complicate

///

As if the act of speaking
were enough (emerging from

a row of trees the lake within the book // the book
continuing—an opening

through which
the house (alone

in a row of
homes, the street existing—

is not enough,
these people—No matter. I

am going out beyond
the garden, grave. Here,

where I am, there,
where you are

ebbing forward,
falling back. To place the next

locality, another form
of weather. Turning inward,

outward. What the forest is
without the word

for forest. A landscape happening
beneath //the waves (the book a landscape happening

///

Do you remember? Once we walked into the wilderness and waited. I was afraid. Your body was a book of margins, opening and closing. The field was there. As when I placed myself beside you, finally, a lake of errant light through which to know the world is not precisely what we prayed for. Such terror there except that I have memories that feel like something else.

Like someone absolutely other
than // and far

V.

ARRANGE EACH PHOTOGRAPH WITH CARE.
THE DEAD ARE HERE, RETURNING.

AFTEREARTH

In the breath of the book before the book and after.
In the blue periphery of after. In the aperture
of speech. In the green infinity of reading,
the bleak community of loss. In the terror

of the margins blossoming.
In the violence of the mind's arrival
blossoming. In the perforated space of utterance.
In the unnamable hallucinations

of the alphabet. In the bright sobriety of awe.
In the illuminated wake of wonder, a world
unfurling in the mute cathedral
of the interior. In the still, uncertain music

of the interior. In the porous borders of the image.
In the dayglow ruins of the dictionary.
In the pregnant lapse of reason.
In the seedling gaps of exposition. In the song-

drawn logic of the dream. In the beautiful
collapse of the house of language.
In the extravagant expanse of the house of language.
In the structure of the garden's darkness,

a mouth in the wilderness, the tongue unraveling.
In the light that isn't light. In the open doorway of the eye

Opening the book and closing it, the word dissolves
in lake-death. We have let it come
to that. To this particular
insistence, a shawl's transparent
winter, the long dark
braid gone down across
your shoulder. When the dress
drops. The word dissolves
in messages like might it not be necessary
to drown your hands in morning,
milk. Too many nightbirds
cancering the day-air. We go so easily
into the hospitals
of evening. Love, a radiant cacophony.
To withstand the autumn
weight, the easy pretty
country. Waking
up in what, in what
cannot. We make when pressed into a lessening
belief // a greater
lessoning. The world beyond
the word in hindsight. Wouldn't that
be violent also? To follow you, one would have to shadow
out the self, construct a narrow
path of gravel through into the anti-sky,
its error like a working spark. Would that I could give
the violent weather of my lungs
to shake apart your form within the after-presences,
aporia. In which, in which is not. Beneath the quivering intensities

EULOGY WHILE LIVING

If I last long enough to listen,
these dreams of spring I've tucked into a book
will sound the pallid apex
of my lapse. Paint them with me,
daughter, make me
brighter. The earth is dark
as money. Still,
I've got a better singer's rendering of god
inside me: blueprint
of the aftermath, these seeds of grief,
perennial. If I was ever
good to you, or if the lake
in which the night
dissolves returns to you
your name, plant them near me
like the living altar
of a prayer I failed to offer
and teach your girls when they come home
to you like lanterns the porous edge
of every utterance I've sold.
By the time you're old enough to read this,
by the time there isn't time. The song does not belong to us,
forgive me. I want to be remembered

ɪ.)

We have these lives and then we try to speak them. Identity, a deity apart. I was praying in an un-dark grove. The alphabet approached me

2.)

It was, if I recall, a Sunday. The wind was like a dead man blinking.
Was there a river? There was a river

3.)

Bestial in the vowel-ed ground
of mourning, I chose the closest noise and troubled sound upon the water

4.)

The noise was all around me, the weather changing voices in the trees

5.)

Believing in the book, its margins sheared, I took my ear and placed it in my mouth.

The sound I heard unfurled
a new geography. The landscape hardened like a scar

6.)

The landscape hardened like a scar, an interstice of syllables in which I sang
my seeing, saying. A new wind bellowed through me like a century. I trembled
inward, a new September stirring in the battered opening above

7.)

A blue dark settled in the center of my sight, a swarm of nightbirds, the garden
fading out. Sewing closed my mouth, I rested in the violence of a form I pushed
a sentence through and wept.

My weeping blurred within me. A figure
in the distance rising

8.)

Are you my master?

9.)

You are my master

10.)

Acknowledgments

Thank you, Brenda Shaughnessy, for believing in these poems, and Stephanie G'Schwind and everyone else at the Center for Literary Publishing at Colorado State University who gave this book their time.

This book would not be possible without the work, thought, and influence of other writers. Most directly, many of the poems in this collection lean on and draw language and inspiration from John Keats, George Oppen, Emily Dickinson, Lorine Niedecker, Joanna Klink, and Robert Baker. I am, as we all are, indebted to those who came before me.

In the spirit of inheritance, many of the poems in this collection were written expressly for other people.

"Book of Weaponry" is for Julie Carr.

"Ommatidia" is for Ian Wallace.

"Spectacle" is for Cody-Rose Clevidence.

"Book of Talk" is for Nickolas Butler.

"Grove of Meaning" is for Serena Chopra.

"Along Our Mouths, Sing Soft" is for (and was written in collaboration with) Jane Wong, Lilly Lam, and Diana Khoi Nguyen.

"Borderwork" is for Numfon Gulig.

"Eulogy While Living" is for my daughters, Pieta and Tonkhoa.

Thanks is also due to the editors and publishers of *The Volta, Spoon River Poetry Review, Denver Quarterly,* and *Wisconsin People & Ideas,* where some of these poems were published in earlier versions or under different names. In particular,

"Field of Book," "Destroyer," the "Pray/Tell" series, "Some Mythologies," "Book of Lake," and "Post-Script" are revised excerpts from the chapbook *Book of Lake*, originally published by *CutBank*.

Thank you to the Wisconsin Academy of Sciences, Arts and Letters; the Academy of American Poets; and the Wisconsin Poet Laureate Commission for your support. Thanks, too, to the many other organizations including but not limited to Woodland Pattern, the Wisconsin Fellowship of Poets, the Wisconsin Humanities Council, the Arts + Literature Laboratory, and the Chippewa Valley Writers Guild, who do so much to cultivate and care for the literary culture of our state.

Thank you also to Karl Gartung, Jenny Penberthy, and the Friends of Lorine Niedecker.

Abiding love to my Wisconsin friends and community, especially Barrett Swanson, Meghan O'Gieblyn, Adam Fell, Caryl Pagel, and the Royaleers Record Club.

For believing in the future, thank you Mary and Roger Rowin.

An endless amount of gratitude is due to my mother and late father, to my sister and her family, and to my uncle, Anthony Gulig.

Finally, and most of all, I am forever indebted to my wife and daughters. My life belongs to your life. This book belongs to you.

This book is set in Caslon and Agency
by The Center for Literary Publishing
at Colorado State University.

Copyediting by Natalia Sperry.
Proofreading by Josephine Gawtry.
Book design and typesetting by Chase Cate.
Cover art by Jason DeMarte.
Cover design by Stephanie G'Schwind.
Printing by Books International.